Bonding: Infantile and Parer

TROWBRIDGE COLLEGE

Mart...

The PACTS series: *Parent, Adolescent and Child Training Skills*

1.   Assessing Children in Need and Their Parents
2.   ABC of Behavioural Methods
3.   Bonding: Infantile and Parental Attachments
4.   Coping with Children's Feeding Problems and Bedtime Battles
5.   Toilet Training, Bedwetting and Soiling
6.   Social Skills Training for Children
7.   Setting Limits: Promoting Positive Parenting
8.   Feuding and Fighting
9.   Banishing Bad Behaviour: Helping Parents Cope with a Child's Conduct
      Disorder
10.   Supporting Bereaved and Dying Children and Their Parents
11.   Separation and Divorce
12.   Post-Traumatic Stress Disorder in Children

Bonding: Infantile and Parental Attachments

by
Martin Herbert

BPS BOOKS

THE BRITISH
PSYCHOLOGICAL
SOCIETY

First published in 1996 by BPS Books (The British Psychological Society), St Andrews House, 48 Princess Road East, Leicester LE1 7DR, UK.

A catalogue record for this book is available from the British Library.

ISBN 1 85433 196 5

Typeset by Ralph Footring, Derby.

Printed in Great Britain by Stanley L. Hunt Printers Ltd., Rushden, Northants.

Contents

Introduction   1
     Aims   1
     Objectives   1

PART I: INFANTILE ATTACHMENTS   3
Infant-to-parent attachments   3
Substitute care   4

PART II: INFANT ATTACHMENT PATTERNS   7
Assessing the quality of child–parent attachments   7
     Maternal sensitivity   8

PART III: PARENTAL BONDING   10
Measuring and assessing bonding   11
The bonding doctrine   12
     The influence of ethology   13
The evidence   15
     Practical implications   17
Measuring parental attachment   18
     Learning to be a mother   18
Fostering and adoption   19
     Exposure learning   19
The baby with physical or mental disabilities   20
Paternal bonding   20

References   23

NOTE TO APPENDICES   24

APPENDICES
I: Responsiveness to the infant   25
II: Parent–infant interaction   27
III: Parental Checklist (school-age period)   28
IV: Common symptoms of
     Reactive Attachment Disorder (RAD)   29

HINTS FOR PARENTS   30

Bonding: infantile and parental attachments

Introduction

Aims

The aims of this guide are to provide the practitioner with the means to assess parental bonding and infantile attachments.

Objectives

In order to fulfil these aims, the guide provides the practitioner with:

- a brief account of the contentious issues surrounding maternal bonding;
- a brief description of infantile attachments;
- the evidence for and against the 'critical period' doctrine of maternal bonding;
- a proforma to describe and rate parental attachment behaviours and attitudes;
- a checklist of symptoms associated with attachment difficulties.

All infants need to become attached to a parent (or parent substitute) in order to survive. The child's growing bond of love and loyalty is a great source of joy to the mother and father, but such ties of affection also serve a utilitarian function. The accompanying respect and goodwill enhances all the adults' efforts to teach them (this applies to teachers as well). The fact that children identify with their parents and are 'on their side', so to speak, makes the task of teaching – and learning – much easier.

The other side of bonding is the parents' commitment to their offspring. When all goes well – and it usually does – an attachment is cemented between the mother (say) and her baby, a relationship implying unconditional love, self-sacrifice and nurturant attitudes which, for the mother's part, are quite likely to last a lifetime. Obviously a great deal is at stake in the success of attachment processes – be they child-to-parent or parent-to-child (see the assessment forms at the back of this guide).

Love is surely one of the most elusive words in the language. There are many kinds of love: a mother's love for her child (often assumed to be synonymous with the term 'maternal bond'); the child's love for its parents; the love between adults, and a child's love for a sibling. In each case of love mentioned (and in most others), love is but a part of one individual's feelings of affection which may be experienced as liking, caring, protecting or sensitivity for another person.

It is important at the outset to draw a clear distinction between *infantile attachment* and *maternal attachment*. Ducklings, goslings and chicks, although normally attached to their natural mother, can easily become attached (if exposed very early in their life) to a foster parent, or, in the laboratory, to a moving inanimate object. This type of early learning is known as *imprinting*. The newborn of mammalian species, capable of locomotion soon after birth (as are most herbivores such as horses, cattle or deer) also appear to form attachments by exposure to figures in their immediate environment, normally their mothers. Regardless of how it is acquired, the specific attachment of a young animal to a particular adult or adult-substitute is known as *infantile attachment*. Naturally, just as an infant can be attached to its mother, so parents become attached to their infant or infant-surrogate. This type of attachment is known as *maternal* or *paternal bonding*.

At the very foundation of normal development is the child's emotional tie to his/her parents and their bonding to him/her. Erik Erikson (1965) proposes that the essential task of infancy is the development of a basic trust in others. He believes that during the early months and years of life, a baby learns whether the world is a good and satisfying place to live, or a source of pain, misery, frustration and uncertainty. Because human infants are so totally dependent for so long, they need to know that they can depend on the outside world.

The development of a sense of trust in the world, derived from parental affection and the prompt satisfaction of need, is a major task. Mistrust and a sense of insecurity are therefore the emotional problems which, potentially, have their origins in the neglect of children's needs during this phase of life. If parents are rejecting and neglectful, the child may see the world not as a manageable and benign place, but as threatening and insecure. Let us therefore look at that all-important bond of love.

Part I: Infantile attachments

Infant-to-parent attachments

Behaviour which is characteristic of infantile attachment may readily be observed in its many forms in human children, as well as in the young of birds and non-human mammals, including infra-human primates such as monkeys and apes. They all show strong ties to their mothers and sometimes also to other individuals, although it is a matter of debate whether those attachments can be ascribed mainly to imprinting-like *exposure learning*.

There is a vast literature on the subject of the affectional ties of human infants to their parents, particularly in the context of *maternal deprivation*. The most influential writings have been those of John Bowlby (1980; 1982). In the briefest outline, his view was that a child's strong attachment to its mother was necessary for normal, healthy development.

The beginning of babies' separate or independent existence takes place at birth, when they cease to receive all sustenance through the umbilical cord. Newborns are genetically programmed to respond in certain ways to the world around them; that is, they are born with a particular type of physical and psychological equipment which makes them sensitive to certain kinds of stimulation in their surroundings. For example, the human face in movement triggers a smile in young babies, and under normal circumstances, the baby's smile – more than anything else – binds a mother to her child with a deep feeling of joy and love. Babies attract and keep their parents' attention by crying, smiling, babbling and laughing. And the more attention they get, the more they want and work for.

We can only speak of a child as a person when s/he becomes aware of her/himself as a separate individual, a social being. Later, to become a person in their own right, they must detach themselves, at least in part, from their mother's protective cocoon and develop a point of view of their own. Like a spaceship which has to force itself out of the earth's gravitational pull in order to make its journey, children must move out of safe orbit around their mothers and strike out to find their own place in the world.

By about four months old, infants generally behave in much the same friendly way towards people as they did earlier, but will react more markedly to their mother. They will smile and coo and follow her with their eyes more than they will other people. But although they may be able to recognize her, the bond has not yet developed which makes them behave in such a way as to maintain close proximity *to her in particular* – the real meaning of attachment. Attachment behaviour is best demonstrated when the mother leaves the room and the baby cries or tries to follow her; it is also evident when not just anyone can placate the infant. At six months about two thirds of babies appear to have a close attachment to their mothers, indicated by separation protests of a fairly consistent sort. Three quarters of babies are attached by nine months. This first attachment is usually directed at the mother, and only very occasionally towards some other familiar figure.

During the months after children first show evidence of emotional bonds, one quarter of them will show attachment to other members of the family, and by the time they are a year and a half old, all but a few children will be attached to at least one other person (usually the father), and often to several others (usually older children). The formation of additional attachments progresses so rapidly in some infants that multiple attachments occur at about the same time. By one year of age the majority of children will show no preference for either parent, and only a few retain their mother-centredness.

Rudolph Schaffer (1977) writes that the child, by his first birthday:

> ... has learned to distinguish familiar people from strangers, he has developed a repertoire of signalling abilities which he can use discriminatively in relation to particular situations and individuals, and he is about to acquire such social skills as language and imitation. Above all, he has formed his first love relationship: a relationship which many believe to be the prototype of all subsequent ones, providing him with that basic security which is an essential ingredient of personality.

Substitute care

Good daycare need not interfere with normal mother–child bonding and the use of day nurseries does not appear to have any long-term adverse psychological or physical effects. Children of working parents are no more likely to develop emotional problems or turn into delinquents than children whose mothers stay at home. It is a commonly held belief (which can be very worrying to parents) that infants who are deprived of *continuous maternal care and love* — undoubtedly evidenced in the history of some older children who are emotionally disturbed — are invariably affected adversely in their ability to form bonds of affection, and in other ways as well.

Bowlby's later view, following an examination of further research findings, was that the child's separation from its caretaker did not inevitably result in the maladjustment of the child; but at the same time, a long-lasting absence of a mother-figure before the age of about five years did greatly interfere with the child's healthy psychological development. The debate concerning infantile attachment and maternal deprivation has continued. Since about 1970 some very useful general appraisals of maternal deprivation effects have become available, as well as of current theories of infantile attachment.

It is instructive to consider, if only very briefly, some practical consequences of the Bowlbian view. Some were benign; others less so! Since child-to-parent uninterrupted attachment was seen as very important for the psychological wellbeing of the child, the impact of child–parent separations had to be, whenever possible, minimized. Accordingly, from the 1950s onwards, children's wards in hospitals were opened to visiting relatives. Previously, it had been believed that sick children who saw their parents became unnecessarily upset. The new view was that it would be better for children to show emotion than to be quietly miserable through continued separation from their loved ones. Thus, the apparent harshness of hardly allowing children in hospital to receive visitors was done away with.

The positive influence of Bowlby, Spitz, and others expressing similar views also extended into another sphere. Earlier on, children in institutional care had been herded together in large establishments, each catering for perhaps hundreds of children. The new ideas demanded that the size of the institutions be drastically reduced. Children were now being put into family-sized cottage homes, each run jointly by a foster mother and a foster father. In time it was realized that the appalling damage to young children so vividly described by Spitz (1946) was not the result of maternal deprivation as such but was due to lack of personal contact and stimulation in bad institutions.

However, side-by-side with these social improvements, certain less desirable developments were in evidence. During the Second World War, nurseries for pre-school children were established to enable mothers to contribute to the war effort in factories, offices and elsewhere. Now, since separation from the mother was thought to be undesirable for young children, war-time nurseries were being closed down. This penalized some youngsters, depriving them of enriching experiences outside the home. It also greatly inconvenienced those mothers who still went to work and who now had to make their own private, and often less adequate, arrangements for child minding. Many parents among the better-educated tended to think that even short mother–infant separations could harm their children psychologically. Such mothers felt anxious or guilty whenever they had to leave their children for a day or so, and were reluctant to make arrangements for substitute care. As a result of continuing research, we nowadays consider that the mother's anxiety and guilt feelings are unnecessary and that well-run nurseries for young children have a very valuable role to play in a modern society. An investigation of working mothers showed that the only children to suffer were those who were sent from pillar to post in a succession of unsatisfactory and unstable child-minding arrangements. They tended to be attention-seeking and clinging.

Part II: Infant attachment patterns

Assessing the quality of child–parent attachments
(see Ainsworth, 1973; Bakeman and Brown, 1977)

Mary Ainsworth and her colleagues (1978) have examined the relationship between the infant's response to separation and reunion and the behaviour of both mother and child in the home environment. The findings suggest that *maternal sensitivity* is most influential in affecting the child's reactions.

Individual infants can be assessed for the quality of their attachments to parents. This assessment is based on their behaviour throughout pre-separation, separation and reunion with their parents. Although Ainsworth emphasizes that multiple criteria are necessary in evaluating infant-to-mother attachments, the so-called 'strange situation' proved to be a particularly useful indicator. It exposed a child to three potentially distressing situations: separation from the mother, contact with a stranger, and unfamiliar surroundings. These took place in eight experimental episodes. It was found that the assessment of infant-to-parent attachment could be described in terms of four broad categories of the infant's response to the presence and absence of the mother (adapted from Ainsworth's work; see Browne and Herbert, 1996; Herbert, 1993):

➤ **Anxious avoidant infants** (Insecurely Attached Type I): show high levels of play behaviour throughout and tend not to seek interaction with the parent or stranger. They do not become distressed at being left alone with the stranger. On reunion with their parent, they frequently resist her physical contact or interaction.

➤ **Independent infants** (Securely Attached Type I): demonstrate a strong initiative to interact with their parent and to a lesser extent, the stranger. They do not especially seek physical contact with their parent and are rarely distressed on separation. They greet their parent upon reunion by smiling and reaching for her.

➤ **Dependent infants** (Securely Attached Type II): actively seek physical contact and interaction with their parent. They are usually distressed and often cry when left alone with the stranger. On their parent's return, they reach for her and maintain physical contact, sometimes by resisting her release. Generally they exhibit a desire for interaction with the parent in preference to the stranger.

➤ **Anxious/resistant or ambivalent infants** (Insecurely Attached Type II): show low levels of play behaviour throughout and sometimes cry prior to separation. They demonstrate an obvious wariness of the stranger and intense distress at separation. They are also more prone to crying while left alone with the stranger. They are ambivalent and frequently mix contact-seeking behaviours with active resistance to contact or interaction. This is especially evident on the parent's return: on reunion, these infants continue to be distressed as usually the parent fails to comfort them.

Maternal sensitivity

In the homes of the securely attached infants, sensitive mothering was exhibited to the infant's behaviour. While insecurely attached, anxious and avoidant infants were found to be rejected by their mothers in terms of interaction, it was suggested that the enhanced exploratory behaviours shown by these infants were an attempt to block attachment behaviours which had been rejected in the past. In the home environments of the insecurely attached anxious and resistant infants a disharmonious and often ambivalent mother–infant relationship was evident. The resistant and ambivalent behaviours shown were seen to be the result of inconsistent parenting.

Maccoby (1980) is of the opinion that the parents' contribution to attachment can be assessed and identified within four dimensions of caretaking style:

➤ **Sensitivity/insensitivity.** The sensitive parent meshes his/her responses to the infant's signals and communications to form a cyclic turn-taking pattern of interaction, whereas the insensitive parent intervenes arbitrarily, and these intrusions reflect his/her own wishes and mood.

➤ **Acceptance/rejection.** The accepting parent accepts in general the responsibility of child care, demonstrating few signs of irritation with the child. The rejecting parent, on the other hand, has feelings of anger and resentment that eclipse his/her affection for the child, often finding the child irritating and resorting to punitive control.

➤ **Co-operation/interference.** The co-operative parent respects the child's autonomy and rarely exerts direct control. The interfering parent imposes his/her wishes on the child with little concern for the child's current mood or activity.

➤ **Accessibility/ignoring.** The accessible parent is familiar with his/her child's communications and notices them at some distance, hence s/he is easily distracted by the child. The ignoring parent is preoccupied with his/her own activities and thoughts. S/he often fails to notice the child's communications unless they are obvious through intensification. S/he may even forget about the child outside the scheduled times for caretaking.

These dimensions are inter-related and together they determine how warm the parent is to the child and what the possibility of rejection is. The implications of parental rejection and appropriate interventions with emotionally abused and neglected children are discussed in Iwaniec (1995). This issue brings us neatly to the next topic: parental bonding.

Part III: Parental bonding

Every so often a psychological theory escapes the confines of sober academic debate associated with professional conferences or learned journals, and enters the wider public arena (and consciousness) by way of extensive publicity in the mass media. In relatively recent times, the theory of maternal bonding has enjoyed (or suffered) the some-what unrestrained discussion characterized, in earlier decades, by the notion of 'maternal deprivation'. What is the reader or viewer – especially the expectant young mother – to make of the interesting but also sometimes disturbing ideas surrounding this concept of a maternal bond?

Much of the thinking about bonding has been preoccupied with maternal attachment, and it has been influenced by, and confused with, research into attachment between the infant and mother. In this work, *proximity seeking* has commonly been utilized to index attach-ment; not surprisingly it also finds its way into key measures of maternal attachment. Behaviours which imply close contact, such as smiling, face presentations, cuddling, kissing, vocalizing, and prolonged gazing, are taken as indices of bonding. Research workers have tended to focus specifically on the mother's behaviour (for example, touching, cuddling), recording the amount of time spent in such activities, and in doing so, they have neglected the contribution of the other member of the dyad – the infant. To parody that old song 'It takes two to tango', it takes two to interact and bond.

Babies' response to their world is much more than a simple reaction to their environment. They are actively engaged in attempts to organize and structure their world. Parents are not the sole possessors of power and influence within the family. What is being suggested is that interactional sequences of mother–child, child–mother behaviours are likely to provide a better measure of the parent–infant relationship than a one-sided account. The notion of a dialogue (or 'conversation') between two individuals has been used as an indicator of the quality of attachments and gives rise to a definition of 'good' relationships expressed in terms of the reciprocity of interactions between the partners. Both mother and child are active concurrently, each for part of the time. The 'good' mother is *responsive* to her baby and continues to respond until s/he is satisfied; she also *initiates* activity with her infant (that is to say, she is **proactive!**).

According to the American paediatricians, Klaus and Kennell (1976), the intimate mother–infant contact in the postpartum sensitive period gives rise to a host of innate behaviours; in their own words, 'a cascade of reciprocal interactions begins between mother and baby (which) locks them together and mediates the further development of attachment'.

Measuring and assessing bonding

Opinions differ about what constitutes maternal attachment. Bonding certainly implies a special and focused relationship towards the mother's own offspring. But what is this quality of specialness? One criterion might be the mother's own report of her attitudes and feelings towards the infant. Indeed, interviews and self-rating scales have been used to this purpose. The mother is adjudged 'attached' to the infant if she consistently, over an extended period of time, reports that she loves her child, feels responsible for it, and has a sense of their mutual belonging. Conversely, the markers for an absence of bonding might be maternal reports of detachment, indifference or hostility towards the baby, and of having a sense of the child being a 'stranger', or separate from her emotionally.

This is all very well, but after all, actions speak louder than words. Observers might be more impressed by a mother's behaviour than by her rhetoric. By this token, a mother would be considered to be 'bonded' to her infant if she looked after him/her well (being aware of the child's needs and responding to them), gave him/her considerable and considerate attention, and demonstrated her love in the form of 'kissing, cuddling, and prolonged gazing'.

Mother-to-infant attachment is usually inferred, in the scientific literature on bonding, from *observations* of just such behaviour, and additionally smiling, vocalizing, touching and face presentations. The trouble with these indices is that they belong to a range of so-called 'infant-elicited social behaviours' which are not only displayed naturally by caregivers, almost at a level of unawareness, but also by many strangers. They tend to occur together in one co-ordinated package. The mother performs a facial display, while vocalizing, while gazing, and within the framework of a discrete head movement coupled with a face presentation. The fact that most women have a predilection to indulge in these pleasant, indeed affectionate, rituals – to smile, touch and tickle *other* people's babies when they meet them – despite there being no question of their being bonded to them, tends to undermine their significance as indicators of attachment.

Our assumptions about what constitute the outward and visible signs of 'good maternal attachment' is likely to bias what we see and select from a mass of observations. The problem of specification of maternal bonding is like the proverbial elephant: difficult to define, but we like to think that we know one when we see one. Inherent in this frivolous observation is a serious problem of reification which misleadingly tends to give 'maternal attachment' the attributes of an *unidimensional entity*. It is made to sound like a mechanical thing – the working of a kind of affectional superglue which will only 'take' if applied at the appropriate time and in the appropriate manner. If successful, the mother (and the emphasis, as we have seen, is exclusively on the mother in the unrestrained view of bonding) is 'tied' or 'stuck' figuratively to her offspring. This mechanical model seems to suggest an all-or-nothing phenomenon.

There is, in fact, no evidence that caring is really like that; it seems more likely to involve several dimensions of nurturance. In other words, each of these somewhat diverse features of caring is a matter of degree (that is, it is measurable along a continuum). Dunn and Richards (1977) set out, in a longitudinal study of 77 mother–child pairs (from birth to five years), to see if a number of categories of behaviours that have been used as indices of affection did, indeed, intercorrelate. Correlations between measures were not high, and they were unable to demonstrate a unitary attribute reflecting 'warm' mothering.

The bonding doctrine

The bonding doctrine is concerned with the contact between the newborn infant and its mother and the long-term influence of this on the mother-to-infant attachment.

Put briefly, this doctrine proposed that in some mammalian species, including our own, mothers become bonded to their infants through close contact -- for example, skin-to-skin – during a short critical period, soon after birth. This is an awesome claim, considering that no other adult human behaviour, and a complex pattern of behaviour and attitude at that, is explained in such 'ethological' terms. To spell it out, the suggestion is that sensory stimulation from the infant soon after its delivery is essential if the mother is to fall in love with her baby. During the critical hours following birth, tactile, visual and olfactory stimulation of the mother by her baby is thought to be particularly significant. Where the mother's initial responsiveness is disrupted by separation (to take one example) there is a risk – it is feared – of long-term adverse consequences for the mother–child relationship. Adverse effects on mother–child bonding are thought to have further repercussions in the form of behavioural symptoms in the child. Some clinicians refer to this as *Reactive Attachment Disorder*, (see *Appendix IV*). See attached

The close-contact, critical-period bonding theory is said to be justified on two grounds. One is rooted in studies of animal behaviour, while the other has to do with observation of human mothers, comparing those who have had little or no contact with their newborn babies with those who have had extended contact.

It will not surprise the reader that the care-giving precepts inherent in the bonding view are but a relatively recent stage in the long history of ideas and practices of child care. From time to time new thoughts on the handling of neonates and new practices have emerged. Yet with the passing of time new ideas become old-fashioned; they fade away, perhaps to reappear later in new guises, they undergo reformulations, they alter in their emphases, they re-emerge, they go out of fashion again.

Most briefly put, the view of maternal bonding is that immediately after the birth of her baby the mother must be made to hold and cuddle it in order to become emotionally tied to the baby; for if she is not, her bond or attachment to the child will be inadequate, which could have harmful long-lasting consequences. These ideas influence day-to-day practice in maternity hospitals, homes and nurseries; they influence decisions made in courts of law (for example, whether a child is to be taken away from its parents, or which of the contesting parents is to be given custody); they influence the advice to young mothers given by doctors, nurses and social workers; they influence what young mothers think and do and feel.

The influence of ethology

With regard to the human species, the last decade has witnessed a growing interest in the possibility that the development of mother-to-infant attachment (indexed by specific actions which serve to indicate affection and focused concern for the infant) is influenced by biological factors. The mother needs to be, as it were, bonded to her infant; her affection for her infant is treated by some writers as something she has to acquire over a limited period of time after the child's birth.

Reading the literature on mother-to-child attachment induces a sense of *déjà vu*. The various preoccupations with the unidimensionality of attachment behaviour, its biological basis, the existence of a sensitive or critical period for the formation of attachments, the dangers of separation of mother and infant, are all reminiscent of the conjectures relating to the maternal deprivation hypothesis. John Bowlby (1980; 1982) whose views have been so influential (and, sadly, so often misunderstood or misrepresented) in the areas of attachment theory and maternal deprivation, emphasizes that the baby's signals of (*inter alia*) distress, elicit the mother's comforting response. The crying and maternal response are thought to have a biological function; they serve as constituents of a system of behaviour binding child and mother closely together.

Bowlby stresses the way in which the behaviour that attaches mother and child resembles that of infra-human primates; he points to the survival value of systems that ensure close proximity and contact between infant and mother during the long period of immaturity of all the apes, and, indeed, humans. Bowlby sees the young baby's crying as one of five *in-built* signals (crying, smiling, sucking, following and clinging) which, given the appropriate reaction of the mother, ensure physical closeness. His notion of the sensitive mother assumes a neat fit between the needs of the baby and the performance of the mother. Not only is the baby's behaviour in-built, but the mother is seen as genetically programmed to respond to the signals. She is biologically attuned as a member of her species to them. This maternal sensitivity is thought to be critical for the development of a stable and happy relationship.

It is interesting to see how Bowlby's ideas about attachment in human babies have been transposed to mothers, but moved back in time to a much earlier period in the transactions between infants and their mothers, and the process renamed bonding. In the course of this transposition, many of Bowlby's caveats and strictures with regard to the evidence of mother–child separations, and his revisions of theory concerning the nature of attachment, seem to be overlooked. A stark critical period hypothesis is applied to mother-to-child attachments, most particularly in practice settings, as if it were analogous to infant-to-mother attachment formation. Clearly, what is needed is empirical evidence obtained specifically from studies of mothers' relationships to their offspring. There are various issues to disentangle in the rather confusing literature in this field; there are the separate questions of the time over which bonding takes place (for example, in infancy only or later in life) and the variables (such as physical contact) which facilitate the development of the attachment.

Let us, therefore, examine such evidence as is available. The widespread belief in the rapid bonding of the human mother to her offspring is rooted, in large part, in studies of maternal behaviour in animals.

The evidence

In infra-human mammals, as in human beings, maternal behaviour is not equally directed to all infants of the species, but, on the contrary, tends to focus on the mother's own infants or the mother's adopted infants. It has been said in support of the bonding doctrine that the sensitive postpartum period for mother-to-infant bonding is not a purely human phenomenon, that it occurs in other mammalian species, and should, therefore, be regarded as a widespread biological/ethological characteristic of animal/human behaviour.

The so-called maternal imprinting in sheep and goats has been cited as evidence that mothers in some mammalian species rapidly form strong attachments to their own newly born young. These conclusions are drawn, however, from some early studies which subsequently turned out to require reinterpretation (see Sluckin, Herbert and Sluckin, 1983). The belief in the rapid 'bonding' of the mother to her newborn infant cannot readily be based on work with animals. Although the advocacy of attaching or bonding mothers to their newborn infants nowadays is widespread, the number of empirical studies of humans relevant to this notion is quite small. The earliest reports that mothers who had differing amounts of contact with their babies in the early period after birth showed some differences in later maternal behaviour are inconclusive, since an examination of the data shows that the similarities in the maternal behaviour of both categories of mothers far outweigh the differences.

To bond or not to bond has become a matter of great concern. What will happen if the newborn infant is ill, or hospital arrangements are inflexible so that the baby is separated from its mother during this critical period? Could a chance separation from her baby really put a blight on a mother's love? Could the baby's development be adversely affected? Sadly, this belief about the ties of affection is also quite likely to engender apprehension and pessimism in would-be adoptive parents. The social work and paediatric literature has been full of dire warnings about the consequences of failures or distortions of mother-to-child bonding. They have been blamed for a variety of problems, including unsuccessful adoptions, children's failure to thrive, infantile autism, and, notably, child abuse. Thus, it is not only parents, but people in the medical and helping professions who are concerned about the implications of the bonding theory for the care of rejected, difficult, premature or disabled infants.

The eminently sensible and humane idea of allowing a mother and her new baby to get to know one another by early and frequent interaction becomes oppressive when the permissive 'ought' is replaced by the dogmatic 'must'! It is well to remember that the bonding doctrine is only one of the most recent milestones in the long history of child care precepts and practices. Ideas and pre-scriptions for the early management of children are like fashions, or even fads – they wax and wane.

Our message to the mother who harbours secret fears, lest she has not been properly bonded to her infant is, 'Stop worrying, your anxiety is the result of your acceptance of the bonding doctrine. It was perfectly sensible of you to believe it when no one knew better; but we now know that research findings reveal no critical period for maternal bonding, and these findings strongly indicate that maternal attachment – like child-to-adult attachment – develops in most cases slowly but surely'.

It has been claimed that the maternal deprivation concept serves to legitimize the social arrangement whereby mothers are expected to provide the predominant care for their offspring. Is maternal bonding in this tradition? One would be hard put to find reference to *paternal* bonding. The father, in western society, consistently appears in a role subsidiary to that of the mother–child relationship in the unfolding drama of the child's development. Very little time and energy have been expended in discovering the psychological and sociological ramifications of fatherhood. Indeed, his relationship with his child has been referred to rather dismissively as a 'secondary relationship'. Critiques contrast such views with the dominance of the social stereotype of motherhood as being natural and 'the font of emotional support'. Such ideologies (and they enjoy a long history) have, in their view, transformed pregnancy and birth into a female monopoly. They observe that developmental psychology has a close relationship with social policy and that it provides ideological reinforcement for the stereotype of motherhood. The father tends to be presented as being peripheral; he is accorded the status of genitor and external economic provider supporting the early mother–child bonding.

Practical implications

The practical consequences of the bonding concept for hospital policy have been both beneficial and potentially harmful. In the past, when maternity hospital routine tended to be rigid, mothers were separated from their infants for long periods, not always for good reasons. Currently, in the UK and the USA, more than 90 per cent of all babies are separated from their mothers after birth for at least brief periods. More prolonged separations are likely if the baby has to receive special care or requires intensive care, such as prolonged oxygen therapy with close monitoring. Special care is an eventuality affecting some 14 per cent of all British babies. The policy on many special-care baby units and, indeed, on ordinary maternity wards, was antipathetic to incipient maternal feelings and sensibilities. As early as the turn of the twentieth century, there was clinical comment on the rejection by some mothers of premature infants. The critique of policy by Klaus and Kennell (1976) was a potent influence for change in obstetrical practices at a time when these practices were being criticized by mothers and nurses who objected to the pervasive view that childbirth was the surgical culmination of a nine-month-long illness. The work of these authors provided the scientific support needed to convince the sceptical medical establishment to accept changes that should have been welcomed on humanitarian grounds alone. Many institutions have since attempted to make childbirth an event in which new parents can experience and express the exhilaration and emotional fulfilment that accompanies the transition to parenthood with as little intrusion by medical personnel as possible.

The aim of Klaus and Kennell in their writing and teaching was to minimize the separation of the ill or premature infant and mother, thus reducing the putative risk of a later disorder of maternal bonding. Sadly, present-day obstetric and nursing procedures sometimes provide for skin-to-skin contact between a mother and her newborn at almost any cost, even if the baby is ill and the mother is depressed, exhausted or in pain. The doctrine takes precedence over common sense; sadly neither child's nor parent's best interests are necessarily served by such doctrinaire forcing of the pace, no matter how well-intentioned.

Measuring parental attachment

In the case of infant-to-mother attachment, Ainsworth recommends the use of multiple criteria to describe the way in which such behaviour is organized and manifested. No less should be demanded for mother-to-child attachment. However, the specification of the behaviours describing bonding remains problematic. For the scientist there is no escaping the obligation of trying to operationalize complex concepts and of trying to measure them, no matter how imperfectly (see the proforma at the end of this guide). Appropriate scales of aspects of attachment behaviour and/or attitudes are required. Ideally the scoring should be carried out by observers without any prior knowledge of the mother–child relationship. The investigator must resist the temptation to disregard overt signs of attachment when s/he has already formed the opinion that a particular mother is not genuinely attached to her baby; for in such circumstances it is easy to reject verbal assurances of love, as well as actions normally indicative of maternal bonding, as spurious. Clearly, there are not a few pitfalls in the attempt to assess maternal attachment in its various social contexts.

Learning to be a mother

Human beings would not, perhaps, be very good at mothering without some, or much, learning. We do not really know how capable an entirely untutored mother would be of taking care of her infant, but we guess that she would not be completely helpless. Insofar as she would have *some* ability to look after her infant, her mothering could be called instinctive. Moreover, the human mother's behaviour towards her infant might also be described as instinctive because of her motivational–emotional state at the time. Her motives and feelings cannot be specified in any exact manner. Nevertheless, it is difficult to believe that her propensity to provide caregiving is wholly unconnected with her genetic endowment. There are scientific objections to the use of the word 'instinct', especially in the context of human behaviour, and perhaps a less controversial term is required to highlight the role of the *genetic* contribution to maternal behaviour. Some of those who adopt anti-maternal-instinct stances probably do not quite mean that nature plays no part whatsoever in maternal behaviour. Rather, their message is concerned with day-to-day practice. And the essence of the message is that both the father and the mother should share equally in the 'mothering' of their children, or, as it is nowadays sometimes put, in the process of 'parenting'.

Dr Spock, the famous authority on child care, stresses that it takes time for parents to fall in love with their new baby, that 'love for the baby comes gradually'. The growth of love is partly a function of the parents' sheer *exposure* to their baby. It is also facilitated by the baby's developing repertoire of responses to stimulation – tactile, visual, auditory, and so on.

Over two decades ago, an eminent American psychologist, Harry Harlow (1971), wrote a book about 'learning to love'. Love defies precise definition, but to Harlow it means 'affectional feelings for others'. As Harlow puts it, 'mother love is indiscriminate, and in human mothers, often absent at the outset'. Specific love tends to develop slowly but surely. The bond to the child gradually grows stronger and stronger. Very, very much later it may weaken, but it probably never vanishes . We may say in passing that the course of the growth of paternal love appears to be essentially similar; but we shall have a little more to say about this later.

Fostering and adoption

Commonsense should reassure us that there is something wrong with maternal bonding theory, or at least the 'fundamentalist' version of it. If it were correct, it would hardly be possible for foster or adoptive parents to form warm attachments to their charges, whom they may not have seen as babies at all. It could be said that it is possible to look after children satisfactorily without ever becoming attached to them, but how many adoptive or foster parents would say that they felt no bond with their child? Tragic 'tug of love' cases have occurred because foster parents have grown so fond of the children in their care that it becomes unbearably hurtful to hand them back to their natural parents.

Exposure learning

The mother's mere exposure to her baby makes a contribution towards the development of a bond to the baby. We may go further and say that exposure, although not the only factor in attachment, is probably the central one. This is a view that emerges from studies of exposure learning. Somewhat surprisingly, perhaps, the evidence is that liking for anybody and anything is initially a direct function of familiarity.

The central feature of exposure learning is that the individual, animal or human, forms an attachment to a given figure, not because s/he is rewarded for it, but because the attachment is, as it were, self-rewarding. This is not to say that external reinforcement of attachment is ineffective. External rewards strengthen attachments, but are not a *sine qua non*. Mere exposure is enough. A foster mother, for example, may be paid for her services and may be praised if her charges thrive; this may help her to develop positive feelings towards her foster children. But an adoptive mother's care for her children might get no such clear reinforcements, and yet she may come to love her children dearly.

The baby with physical or mental disabilities

The question of bonding sometimes arises when mothers have to cope with special problems in caring for handicapped children. Skin-to-skin contact soon after birth is no more relevant to the acceptance or otherwise of a baby with physical or mental disabilities than it is to a non-disabled infant. Helping the family to accept such a baby calls for tactful counselling over a long period, starting when the medical facts have become clearly established. After the initial shock, mothers tend to react in a variety of ways. Whether they initially reject the diagnosis, whether they initially reject the infant, whether they are initially excessively loving, they all tend to ask for more information. Thus, *informed* help is needed to enable the mother and father to cope.

Paternal bonding

The bonding doctrine would seem to imply that paternal love is of a different order and quality from maternal love. The fact that a female gives birth does not necessarily mean that she invariably cares for the baby. This is so even in some animal species; male marmosets, to take one example, carry the infant at all times except when the infant is feeding. There have been variations among human groups. Anthropologists tell us that children may not be the special responsibility of their parent at all in some societies; they may be reared by all the members of a group living together under one roof or in a small compact housing unit. Contemporary western society is witnessing a massive increase in the number of single-parent families, in some of which the father is the caregiver.

Fathers, of course, *do* become engrossed in their infants and develop powerful bonds of affection. Commonsense, personal experience, and experimental evidence tell us so, and it happens (in most cases) shortly after birth without the benefit of skin-to-skin contact. Father-to-infant attachment is actually not so different in kind from maternal attachment. Certainly paternal behaviour soon after the birth of a baby very often resembles, in many details, maternal behaviour. Paternal attachment, however, often (but not invariably) appears to be less strong than maternal attachment. There are several suggested reasons for this.

In the first place, general responsiveness of the human male to infants tends to be less marked. It would not altogether surprise us if there were genetic factors responsible for this. In many, but not all, species of primates, males are less nurturing to the young than females, although males tend to be protective both towards the females and their young. Undoubtedly, however, the role of the human male in relation to the young is enormously influenced by culture, custom and convention. Until relatively recent times in Western and Central Europe, men were not expected to perform certain domestic duties, including the feeding of young infants, changing nappies, and so on. The situation in this regard is at present changing rapidly, and it may be that without the cultural overlay, men's feelings and responses towards babies would not be all that different from women's. Given the undoubted changes in social attitudes, researchers have been eager to see whether such changes are skin deep. For example, do babies trigger the same kind of responsiveness in males and females? They usually show men and women films of babies crying and at the same time measure their psychophysiological responsiveness, such as their heart rate and blood pressure. In general, men and women appear to react in similar ways. Second, researchers have examined the ways in which parents greet their newborns since, in many species, parental behaviour is programmed to protect newborns and enhance responsive behaviour toward the young. Again, the similarities outweigh any differences. Most studies find that children do not distinguish between their parents – either can serve as an emotional haven – although there is some evidence to suggest that under severe stress children tend to show a preference for their mothers.

In present day society some men do become highly involved with their children. But in the usual western family, the extent of contact between father and baby is less than that between mother and baby. This may be regrettable, but it is a fact that cannot be overlooked. In these circumstances, paternal attachments have less opportunity to grow at the same rate as maternal attachments. Exposure learning, classical conditioning, operant learning, and imitation have less time to operate. No wonder that paternal attachments often seem less emotional than maternal attachments and dominate men's lives less than they do women's lives. What is perhaps surprising is that, despite everything, the attachments of fathers to their offspring are, for the most part, so extremely strong.

Many fathers make what is really a token effort to keep up with the practical skills of child rearing, concentrating more on becoming good friends to their youngsters. Nevertheless, many have an underlying feeling that their relationships are not on as sound a footing as their partners' maternal bonds. Researchers who have studied the father's contribution to family life conclude that any new father should be encouraged to spend as much time as possible with his partner and child. The most frequent barrier between father and child is the father's work schedule. Many fathers, because of long-term goals, sacrifice time with their families only to find that they have 'lost' their children, at least psychologically, in the process. In some cases, modifications in the daily work routine, if possible, can ensure his fuller participation in his children's care.

References

Ainsworth, M.D.S. (1969). Object relations, dependency and attachment: a theoretical review of the infant–mother relationship. *Child Development, 40,* 969–1025.

Ainsworth, M.D. (1973). The development of infant–mother attachment. In Caldwell, B.M. and Ricciuti, H.N. (Eds) *Review of Child Development Research.* Chicago: University of Chicago Press.

Ainsworth, M.D., Blehar, M.S., Walters, E. and Wall, S. (1978). *Patterns of Attachment.* Hillsdale, NJ: Erlbaum.

Bakeman, R. and Brown, J.V. (1977). Behavioural dialogues – an approach to the assessment of mother–infant interaction. *Child Development, 48,* 195–203.

Bowlby, J. (1980). *Attachment and Loss: Loss.* New York: Basic Books.

Bowlby, J. (1982). *Attachment and Loss: Attachment.* New York: Basic Books.

Browne, K. and Herbert, M. (1996). *Preventing Family Violence.* Chichester: Wiley.

Dunn, J.B. and Richards, M.P.M. (1977). Observations on the developing relationship between mother and baby in the neonatal period. In Schaffer, H.R. (Ed.) *Studies in Mother–Infant Interaction.* London: Academic Press.

Erikson, E. (1965). *Childhood and Society.* Harmondsworth: Penguin.

Harlow, H.F. (1971). *Learning to Love.* San Francisco, CA: Albion.

Harper, L.V. (1975). The scope of offspring effects: from caregiver to culture. *Psychological Bulletin, 82,* 784–801.

Herbert, M. (1993). *Working with Children and the Children Act.* Leicester: BPS Books (The British Psychological Society).

Iwaniec, D. (1995). *The Emotionally Abused and Neglected Child.* Chichester: Wiley.

Klaus, M.H. and Kennell, J.H. (1976). *Maternal–Infant Bonding.* St. Louis: Mosby.

Maccoby, E.E. (1980). *Social Development: Psychology, Growth and the Parent–Child Relationship.* New York: Harcourt Brace Jovanovich.

Schaffer, H. R. (1977). *Mothering.* London: Open University/Fontana.

Sluckin, W., Herbert, M. and Sluckin, A. (1983). *Maternal Bonding.* Oxford: Basil Blackwell.

Spitz, R.A. (1946). Anaclitic depression. *Psychoanalytic Study of the Child, 2,* 313–42.

Note to Appendices

These proformas should help the practitioner to describe and rate the kinds of behaviour and attitude which are commonly thought to indicate parental attachment/bonding. In the case where you are making your own judgements based upon observation, it is critical to reach a conclusion only after seeing a fair, that is, a representative, sample of your client's behaviour in different settings and circumstances.

A necessary precaution: The rating scales and questionnaires designed for use with clients do not provide definitive 'diagnostic' statements about clients and/or their problems. This is especially the case in the areas of child abuse and depression. Nor do the ratings or frequency tallies imply test scores of the kind that are obtained from personality or IQ tests scales. **In other words, they are not strictly speaking numerical scales.** They are designed to help you avoid 'fuzzy', global judgements by making finer assessments which can act as, and should be regarded as, guides only – clues to possible problems (for example, extremely high or low counts) and disorders (unusual or bizarre patterns). They are screening devices, the first stage in the search for further evidence. They also provide markers that will allow you to monitor change in your clients over periods of time. As such, they are ipsative and idiographic, not normative or nomothetic, devices allowing you to indicate by observation or self-report, a person's behaviours, attitudes, feelings, relative to him/herself.

Throughout your assessment, ask yourself:

➤ Is the child's adaptive behaviour appropriate to his/her age, intelligence, cultural context and social situation?
➤ Is the environment making reasonable demands of the child?
➤ Is the environment satisfying the crucial needs of the child; that is, the needs that are vital at his/her particular stage of development?

Appendix I: Responsiveness to the infant

Child's name:
Child's age:
Date:

Base your ratings, for the categories below, on a representative and fair sample of observations.

	Ratings			
Does the caregiver or parent:	Always	Most of the time	Some of the time	Never
Respond promptly to the infant's needs?				
Respond appropriately to his/her needs?				
Respond consistently?				
Interact smoothly and sensitively with the child?				

Prompt responding

Infants have very limited abilities to appreciate the contingencies (association) of events to their own behaviour; an interval of only three seconds is required to disrupt the contingency learning of six-month-old infants. Where the adult takes appreciably longer to answer the infant's signals there will be no opportunity for the child to learn that his/her behaviour can thereby affect his/her environment and in particular the behaviour of other people.

Appropriate responding

This means the ability to recognize the particular messages the infant is trying to communicate, and to interpret and react to them correctly.

Consistency

A child's environment must be predictable; s/he must be able to learn that his/her behaviour will produce particular consequences under particular conditions.

Interacting smoothly

Parents can mesh their interactions with the infant's in a manner that is facilitative and pleasurable as opposed to intrusive and disruptive.

Appendix II: Parent–infant interaction

Child's name:
Child's age:
Date:

Observations *Does the parent do any of the following?*	Yes	No	Don't know
Initiate positive interactions with the infant?			
Respond to the infant's vocalizations?			
Change voice tone when talking to the infant?			
Show interest in face-to-face contact with the infant?			
Show the ability to console or comfort the infant?			
Enjoy close physical contact with the infant?			
Respond to the infant's indications of distress?			

Appendix III: Parental checklist (school-age period)

Does the parent/caregiver:	Always	Usually	Some-times	Seldom	Never
Encourage the child's ideas?					
Listen carefully so as to understand?					
Communicate clearly to the child?					
Respect his/her privacy?					
Set an example for the child?					
Provide guidance at appropriate times?					
Share (family news/appropriate decisions)?					
Respect his/her views?					
Acknowledge the child's efforts?					
Demonstrate emotional support (by comforting or encouraging)?					
Keep confidences?					
Make eye contact during conversation?					
Address the child by name?					
Remember the child's birthday?					
Talk to the child about family matters?					
Discuss (when appropriate) religion, politics, sex, education, death, etc.?					
Teach the child appropriate social skills?					
Accept the child's friends?					
Manage, resolve (fairly) any conflicts between children?					
Set reasonable limits and stick to them?					

Appendix IV: Common symptoms of Reactive Attachment Disorder (RAD)

- ➤ superficially engaging, charming (phoniness)
- ➤ lack of eye contact
- ➤ indiscriminately affectionate with strangers
- ➤ lacking ability to give and receive affection (not cuddly)
- ➤ extreme control problems: often manifest in covert or sneaky ways
- ➤ destructive to self and others
- ➤ cruelty to animals
- ➤ chronic, crazy lying
- ➤ no impulse controls
- ➤ learning lags and disorders
- ➤ lacking cause and effect thinking
- ➤ lack of conscience
- ➤ abnormal eating patterns
- ➤ poor peer relationships
- ➤ preoccupied with fire, blood, gore
- ➤ persistent nonsense questions and incessant chatter
- ➤ inappropriately demanding and clingy
- ➤ abnormal speech patterns
- ➤ passive-aggression: provoking anger in others
- ➤ unusually angry parents

Few children with RAD will exhibit ALL of these symptoms!

Hints for Parents

Many parents tend to think that even short mother–infant separations could harm their children psychologically. Such mothers may feel anxious or guilty whenever they have to leave their children for a day or so, and are reluctant to make arrangements for substitute care. As a result of continuing research, we nowadays consider that these anxiety and guilt feelings are unnecessary and that well-run nurseries for young children have a very valuable role to play in a modern society. An investigation of working mothers showed that the only children to suffer were those who were sent from pillar to post in a succession of unsatisfactory and unstable child-minding arrangements. They tended to be attention-seeking and clinging.

On the whole, children who go (say) to a high quality nursery may stand to gain socially and intellectually by becoming more independent and by coming into contact with other children in day care. Mixing with other children broadens the range of a child's social behaviour – the more they have to adapt to a variety of other individuals, the more their repertoire of social skills will grow. They have the opportunity to learn how to give and take, solve conflicts, and to co-operate. The perennial problem, for many parents and notably single mothers, is to obtain and/or afford high quality substitute care.

The important thing to remember is that a good mother–child relationship does not depend on being together every minute, day in, day out. It depends on what happens between you when you *are* together, and the quality of care given.